U.S. Sites and Symbols

★ ★ ★ ★ ★ ★ ★ ★ ★ ★ ★ ★

Flags

Lauren Diemer

WEIGL PUBLISHERS INC.

Published by Weigl Publishers Inc.
350 5th Avenue, Suite 3304, PMB 6G
New York, NY 10118-0069

Website: www.weigl.com
Copyright ©2009 WEIGL PUBLISHERS INC.

All of the Internet URLs given in the book were valid at the time of publication. However, due to the dynamic nature of the Internet, some addresses may have changed, or sites may have ceased to exist since publication. While the author and publisher regret any inconvenience this may cause readers, no responsibility for any such changes can be accepted by either the author or the publisher.

Library of Congress Cataloging-in-Publishing Data

Diemer, Lauren.
 Flags / Lauren Diemer.
          p. cm. (U.S. sites and symbols)
 Includes index.
 ISBN 978-1-59036-887-9 (soft cover: alk. Paper)—ISBN 978-1-59036-886-2 (hard cover: alk. Paper) 1. Flags—United States—States—Juvenile literature. I. Title.
 CR113.2.D54 2009
 929.9'20973—dc22

2008015826

Printed in the United States of America
1 2 3 4 5 6 7 8 9 0 12 11 10 09 08

Editor: Danielle LeClair
Designer: Kathryn Livingstone

Photograph Credits
Weigl acknowledges Shutterstock, iStockphoto, and Dreamstime as the primary image suppliers for this title. Unless otherwise noted, all images herein were obtained from Shutterstock, iStockphoto, Dreamstime, and their contributors.

Other photograph credits include: Alamy: page 45 (bottom).

Contents

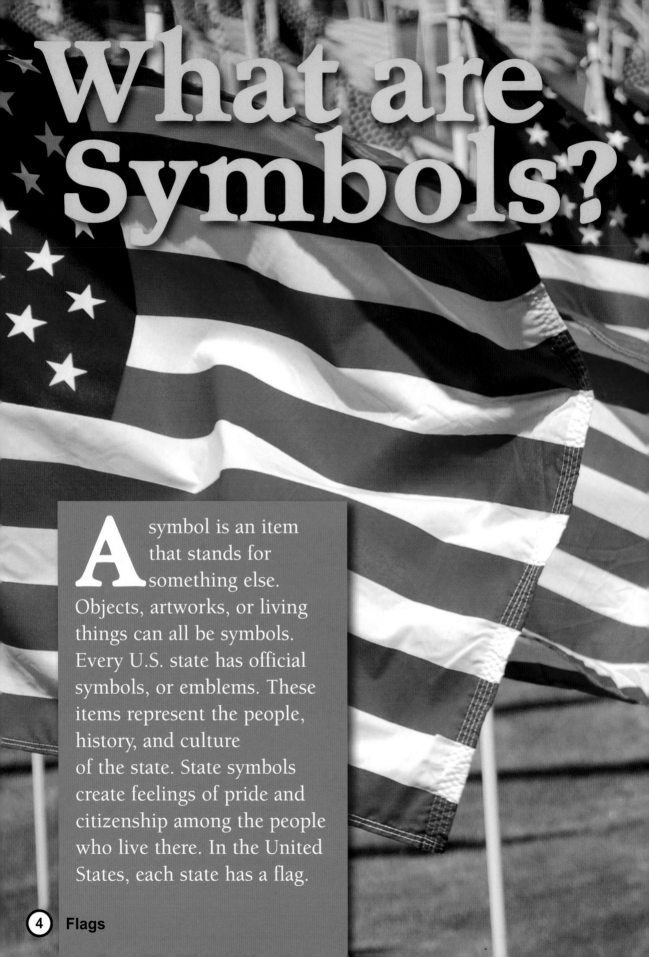

What are Symbols?

A symbol is an item that stands for something else. Objects, artworks, or living things can all be symbols. Every U.S. state has official symbols, or emblems. These items represent the people, history, and culture of the state. State symbols create feelings of pride and citizenship among the people who live there. In the United States, each state has a flag.

State Flag History

The state flag is a symbol of the things that make a state unique. The loyalty and ideals of the people who live in the state are included in the design of the flag. Flags can symbolize many things including events from the state's history. Before 1923, each state had to model its flag after the national flag. Now, each state can design a unique flag, without including parts of the national flag. Often, the state flags contain symbols, pictures, or words that are important to the state. Some states display animals or plants that are unique to the state. Other flags use words to express state pride.

The American flag has changed 26 times since it was adopted in 1775.

Finding State Flags by Region

Alaska

Hawai'i

Washington

Montana

Oregon

Idaho

Wyoming

The West

Nevada

Utah

Colorado

California

Arizona

New Mexico

Each state has a flag symbol. In this book, the states are organized by region. These regions are the West, the Midwest, the South, and the Northeast. Each region is unique because of its land, people, and wildlife. Throughout this book, the regions are color coded. To find a state flag, first find the state using the map on this page. Then, turn to the pages that are the same color as that state.

North
Dakota

Minnesota

South
Dakota

Wisconsin

Michigan

Iowa

The Midwest

Ohio

Nebraska

Indiana

Illinois

West
Virginia

Kansas

Missouri

Kentucky

Virginia

Arkansas

Tennessee

North Carolina

Oklahoma

The South

South
Carolina

Georgia

Texas

Alabama

Mississippi

Florida

Louisiana

New
Hampshire

Vermont

Maine

Massachusetts

The Northeast

New York

Pennsylvania

Rhode
Island

Connecticut

New Jersey

Delaware

Maryland

Web Crawler

Find out facts about each state at
www.americaslibrary.gov. Click on
"Explore the States."

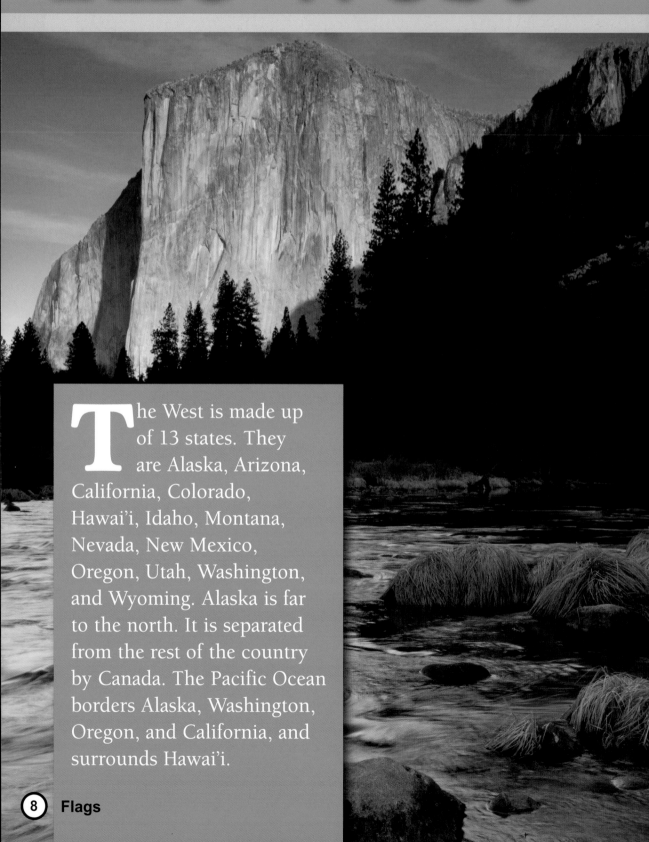

The West

The West is made up of 13 states. They are Alaska, Arizona, California, Colorado, Hawai'i, Idaho, Montana, Nevada, New Mexico, Oregon, Utah, Washington, and Wyoming. Alaska is far to the north. It is separated from the rest of the country by Canada. The Pacific Ocean borders Alaska, Washington, Oregon, and California, and surrounds Hawai'i.

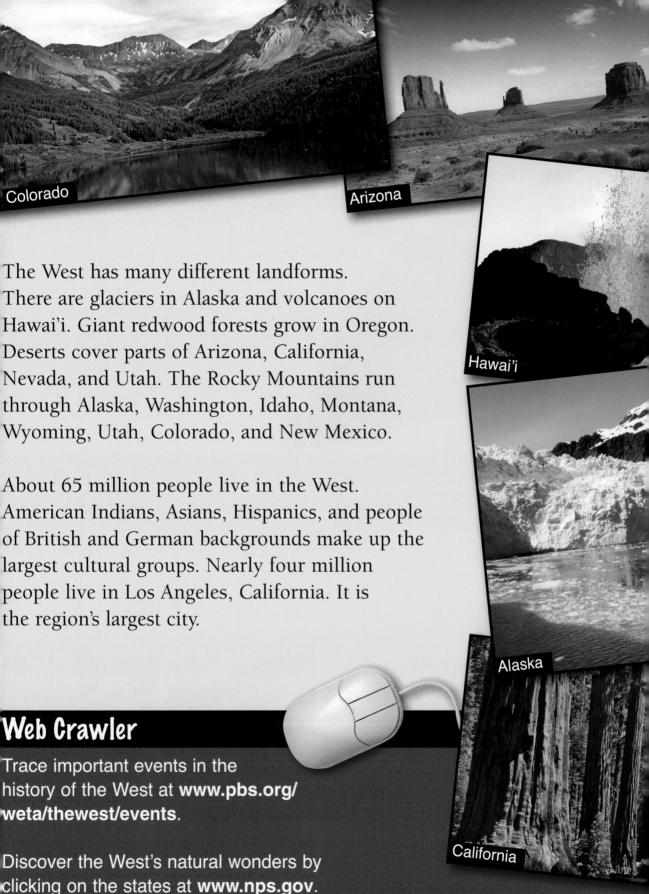

Colorado

Arizona

Hawai'i

Alaska

California

The West has many different landforms. There are glaciers in Alaska and volcanoes on Hawai'i. Giant redwood forests grow in Oregon. Deserts cover parts of Arizona, California, Nevada, and Utah. The Rocky Mountains run through Alaska, Washington, Idaho, Montana, Wyoming, Utah, Colorado, and New Mexico.

About 65 million people live in the West. American Indians, Asians, Hispanics, and people of British and German backgrounds make up the largest cultural groups. Nearly four million people live in Los Angeles, California. It is the region's largest city.

Web Crawler

Trace important events in the history of the West at **www.pbs.org/ weta/thewest/events**.

Discover the West's natural wonders by clicking on the states at **www.nps.gov**.

Alaska

Alaska's state flag is called the "Eight Stars of Gold." The flag was designed in 1927 by an orphan named Benny Benson. The flag he designed has a dark blue background. It also has eight five-pointed gold stars shaped like the **Big Dipper**. A large star represents the pole star, **Polaris**. The flag was adopted in 1959.

Arizona

The state flag of Arizona was adopted on February 17, 1917. The 13 yellow and red rays represent both the Sun's rays and the original 13 colonies of the United States. The colors red and yellow represent the flag of the Spanish **conquistador** Francisco Vasquez de Coronado, who entered Arizona in 1540. The copper-colored star in the center represents the state's copper mining industry.

California

The official state flag of California is called the Bear Flag. It was first used on June 14, 1846, by a group of American settlers who were revolting against the rule of Mexico. The original flag was painted by William Todd. It had a grizzly bear and a five-pointed star above a red bar. The words "California Republic" were placed under the bear. The flag was not officially adopted in 1911.

Colorado

The Colorado state flag was designed by Andrew Carlisle Johnson in 1911. It was adopted on June 5, 1911. Colorado's flag is white, blue, red, and gold. The white in the flag symbolizes Colorado's snowcapped mountains. The blue stands for clear blue skies. The red is for the reddish soil, and the golden yellow represents the Sun.

Hawai'i

The state flag for the Hawai'i was designed in Great Britain in 1798 for King Kamehameha of Hawai'i. Captain George Vancouver brought the flag to the king. The eight stripes of white, red, and blue represent the eight main islands of Hawai'i. The **Union Jack** in the upper right corner shows the close relationship between Hawai'i and Great Britain.

Idaho

The state flag of Idaho was chosen in 1907. The flag is blue with the state seal in the center. The seal was created in 1890 by Emma Edwards Green. She was the only woman to design a state seal. It displays the industries of the state, including mining, agriculture, and forestry, as well as the state's natural beauty.

Montana

Montana's official flag was adopted in 1905. The flag shows the state seal. On the seal is a picture of the Montana landscape. A plow symbolizes the agriculture industry, and a pick and shovel represent mining. A ribbon below the landscape states Montana's motto, *Oro y plata,* which is Spanish for "Gold and Silver."

Nevada

Since 1915, the state flag for Nevada has changed four times. In 1926, the state had a contest to design a new flag. The winner, Louis Schellbach III, won $25 for his design. The "Schellbach" design was adopted in 1929, but a change in where the state name would be placed on the flag was forgotten. In 1991, the mistake was corrected, and Nevada re-adopted the flag.

New Mexico

There have been two versions of New Mexico's state flag. The new version has a red zia in the center of a yellow background. The zia is an ancient symbol of the Sun. New Mexico chose this flag in 1920.

Oregon

Oregon's state flag was adopted in 1925. It is the only state flag that has a design on both sides. The front of the flag has a deep blue background and yellow designs. The back of the flag shows Oregon's official animal, the beaver.

Utah

The Utah state flag was designed for the battleship *Utah* in 1912. It was made the official state flag in 1913. The flag has a beehive, which stand for hard work and industry. It also has a bald eagle and a sego lily, both representing peace.

Washington

Washington adopted its official flag in 1923. The flag has a deep green background with the state seal in the center. The state seal pictures George Washington, the first president of the United States. Washington has the only state flag that pictures a president and has a green background.

Wyoming

On January 31, 1917, the Wyoming state flag was made official. The flag was designed by a Wyoming woman named Verna Keays. The state flag of Wyoming has the same colors as the U.S. national flag. The red border represents the blood of the pioneers who gave their lives for the state. The white is for purity. Justice is symbolized by the blue in the flag.

The Midwest

The Midwest is in the center of the United States. It lies between the Rocky Mountains in the west and the Appalachian Mountains in the northeast. The Ohio River separates the Midwest from the South. Canada lies to the north. There are 12 states in the Midwest. They are Illinois, Indiana, Iowa, Kansas, Michigan, Minnesota, Missouri, Nebraska, North Dakota, Ohio, South Dakota, and Wisconsin.

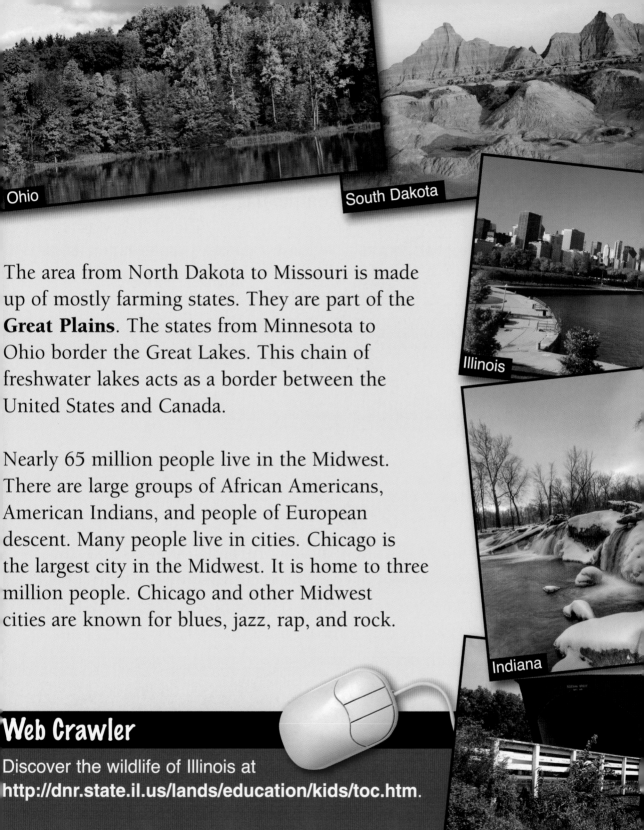

Ohio

South Dakota

Illinois

The area from North Dakota to Missouri is made up of mostly farming states. They are part of the **Great Plains**. The states from Minnesota to Ohio border the Great Lakes. This chain of freshwater lakes acts as a border between the United States and Canada.

Nearly 65 million people live in the Midwest. There are large groups of African Americans, American Indians, and people of European descent. Many people live in cities. Chicago is the largest city in the Midwest. It is home to three million people. Chicago and other Midwest cities are known for blues, jazz, rap, and rock.

Indiana

Web Crawler

Discover the wildlife of Illinois at
http://dnr.state.il.us/lands/education/kids/toc.htm.

Explore a virtual Midwest farmhouse at
www.pbs.org/ktca/farmhouses/vf.html.

Iowa

Illinois

Illinois has had two state flags. The first was adopted in 1915. The **Daughters of the American Revolution** helped in its design. The state name was not on the flag, so in 1970, the flag was redesigned. The official flag was adopted on July 1, 1970, after adding "Illinois."

Indiana

In 1916, when Indiana turned 100 years old, the Daughters of the American Revolution held a flag design competition. The winning design, by Paul Hadley, was approved by the state in 1917. The torch on the flag represents understanding and liberty. Around the torch are rays spreading outward from its flames. A total of 19 stars surround the torch, showing that Indiana was the 19th state to join the Union.

Iowa

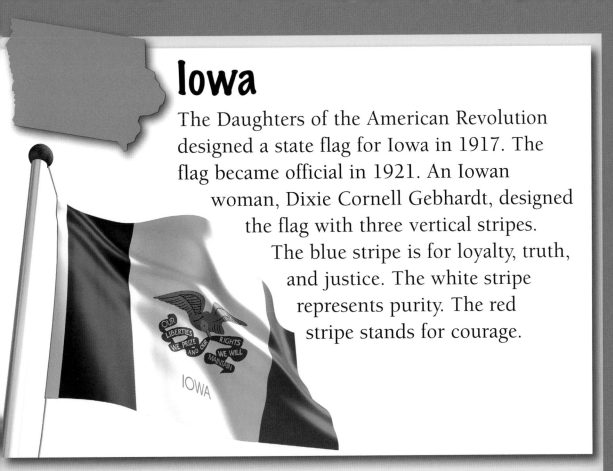

The Daughters of the American Revolution designed a state flag for Iowa in 1917. The flag became official in 1921. An Iowan woman, Dixie Cornell Gebhardt, designed the flag with three vertical stripes. The blue stripe is for loyalty, truth, and justice. The white stripe represents purity. The red stripe stands for courage.

Kansas

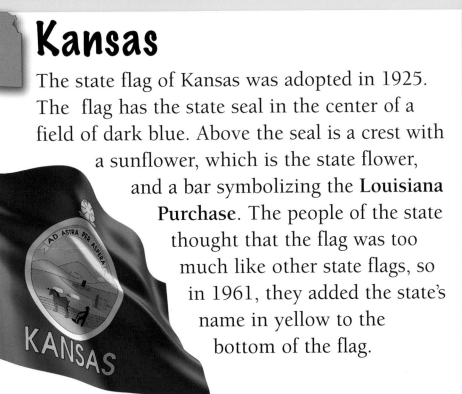

The state flag of Kansas was adopted in 1925. The flag has the state seal in the center of a field of dark blue. Above the seal is a crest with a sunflower, which is the state flower, and a bar symbolizing the **Louisiana Purchase**. The people of the state thought that the flag was too much like other state flags, so in 1961, they added the state's name in yellow to the bottom of the flag.

Michigan

Since becoming a state in 1837, there have been three state flags. The present flag has a coat of arms with an eagle holding an olive branch and arrows. The flag shows an elk and a moose supporting the coat of arms. It also depicts a man standing on a grassy peninsula. This became Michigan's official flag in 1911.

Minnesota

The first state flag of Minnesota was adopted in 1893 and designed by Mrs. Edward H. Center. A new flag was designed and adopted in 1957. The flag is royal blue, fringed in gold, and has 19 stars. The large star represents the North Star and Minnesota. There is a seal in the center of the flag. The French words *l'ètoile du nord*, which means "star of the north," are written in yellow letters on a red banner.

Missouri

Marie Elizabeth Oliver designed the state flag for Missouri in 1908. The flag was adopted on March 22, 1913. There are three large stripes on the flag. The blue strips represents persistence and justice. The red stripe stands for bravery. The white stripe is for purity. Missouri was the 24th state to join the Union, so there are 24 stars around the coat of arms on the flag.

Nebraska

Nebraska's official flag was adopted in 1925. The state seal is on a blue background. The seal contains many symbols that stand for important events in the building and growth of Nebraska. There is a blacksmith holding a hammer. A steamboat moves up the Missouri River, and a train heads toward the Rocky Mountains in the west. The settler's cabin, the wheat, and the stalks of growing corn represent agriculture.

North Dakota

The first flag of North Dakota was adopted in 1911. It is similar to the flag carried by the North Dakota Infantry in the Spanish American War. It is dark blue with a bald eagle carrying an olive branch and arrows. There is a shield on the eagle's breast. The 13 stripes symbolize the 13 original states of the Union.

Ohio

Ohio's official flag was designed by John Eisenmann and adopted in 1902. The flag has three red horizontal stripes and two white horizontal stripes.

There is a blue triangle with 17 five-pointed stars to show that Ohio was the 17th state to join the Union. Ohio's state flag is the only burgee, or a square flag with a swallow-tail.

South Dakota

The original South Dakota flag was designed by Senator Ernest May and Doane Robinson, who was secretary of the State Historical Society. Then in 1969, Will Robinson, Doane Robinson's son, redesigned the flag. The state flag for South Dakota is blue. It has the state seal in the middle. Around the seal is a golden Sun. The words "South Dakota, The Sunshine State" circle the Sun.

Wisconsin

In 1863, the flag of Wisconsin was designed. It became the official flag in 1913. The symbols on the coat of arms are the plow, pick, shovel, arm, hammer, and anchor. These represent Wisconsin's main industries, including manufacturing, agriculture, mining, and shipping. There also is a pyramid of triangles that symbolize bars of iron, called ingots. The ingots stand for the 13 original states.

The South

The South is made up of 16 states. They are Alabama, Arkansas, Delaware, Florida, Georgia, Kentucky, Louisiana, Maryland, Mississippi, North Carolina, Oklahoma, South Carolina, Tennessee, Texas, Virginia, and West Virginia. The Atlantic Ocean borders the South from Delaware to the tip of Florida. A part of the Atlantic Ocean called the Gulf of Mexico stretches from Florida's west coast to Texas. Mexico lies to the south.

Flags

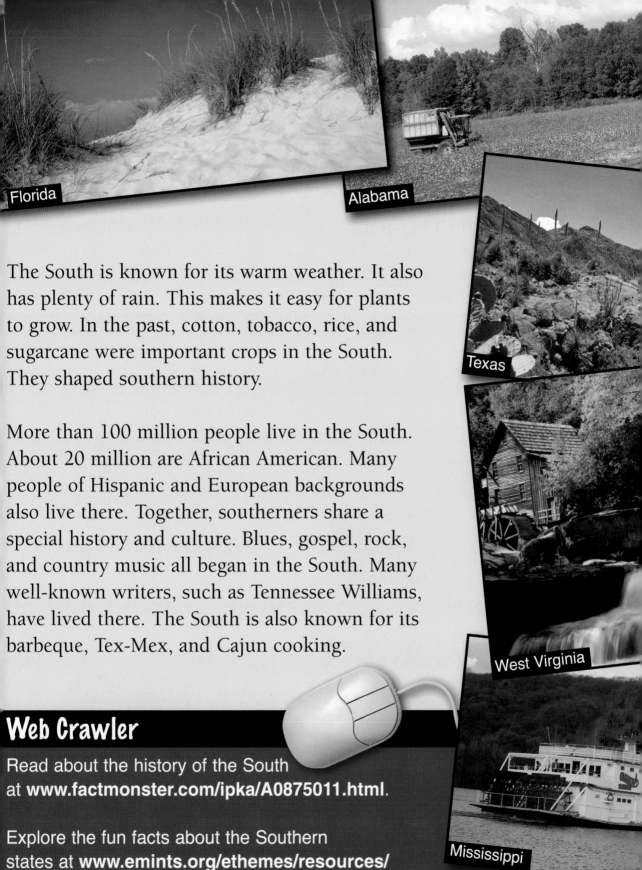

Florida

Alabama

Texas

West Virginia

The South is known for its warm weather. It also has plenty of rain. This makes it easy for plants to grow. In the past, cotton, tobacco, rice, and sugarcane were important crops in the South. They shaped southern history.

More than 100 million people live in the South. About 20 million are African American. Many people of Hispanic and European backgrounds also live there. Together, southerners share a special history and culture. Blues, gospel, rock, and country music all began in the South. Many well-known writers, such as Tennessee Williams, have lived there. The South is also known for its barbeque, Tex-Mex, and Cajun cooking.

Web Crawler

Read about the history of the South at **www.factmonster.com/ipka/A0875011.html**.

Explore the fun facts about the Southern states at **www.emints.org/ethemes/resources/S00000575.shtml**.

Mississippi

Alabama

The official flag of Alabama is called the "crimson cross of St. Andrew's." This flag

was adopted in 1895 and was patterned from the **Confederate Battle Flag**. It can be any type of rectangle or square, but the crimson bars must be 6 inches wide.

Arkansas

In 1926, Arkansas adopted its state flag. The diamond shape in the center of the flag represents the fact that Arkansas is the only state where diamonds have been found. Since Arkansas was the 25th state to join the Union, there are 25 stars around the diamond.

Delaware

The Delaware state flag was adopted in 1913. The colors of the flag are buff, or yellow-brown, and colonial blue. These were the colors of George Washington's uniform during the Revolutionary War.

DECEMBER 7, 1787

Florida

The first Florida state flag was said to look like a white flag of truce, or surrender. It showed the state seal in the center of a white background. The state changed the flag in 1900. They added a red St. Andrew's cross.

Georgia

Georgia has had more flag designs than any other state. The flag kept changing until the 1950s. The Confederate Battle Flag used during the American Revolutionary War was included in the state flag until 1956. Georgia chose its current flag in 2003.

Kentucky

Before 1918, there were many unofficial flags flying over Kentucky. The design of the Kentucky state flag was approved in 1928. It changed again in 1962. These flags included the *fleur de lis* and the Union Jack.

Louisiana

Louisiana's flag was adopted in 1912, 100 years after Louisiana became a state. The coat of arms of the state is placed on a blue background, which represents truth. A picture of a pelican, the state bird, is also on the flag.

Maryland

The flag of Maryland was adopted in 1904. It has the coats of arms of two families, the Calverts and the Crosslands, who founded the state. The Calvert colors are gold and black. The cross **bottony** is a symbol of the Crossland family.

Mississippi

The official flag of Mississippi was adopted in 1894. It has a small Confederate Battle Flag in the upper left corner. There are 13 white stars, representing the original 13 states, on a St. Andrew's cross.

North Carolina

North Carolina did not have a state flag until 1885, which was the year it joined the Union. On the left side of the flag there is a gold wreath and the letters "NC," for North Carolina. The date May 20, 1775 represents when North Carolina declared independance from Great Britain. April 12, 1861 is when North Carolina left the Union to join the Confederate States during the American Revolutionary War.

Oklahoma

The current flag of Oklahoma is the state's 14th flag. This blue flag has a American Indian war shield in the center. There are small crosses on the shield. These crosses are an American Indian design for stars. Seven eagle feathers drop from the edge of the shield. An American Indian peace pipe and an olive branch are together. Both are symbols of peace. The first state flag for Oklahoma was chosen from entries in a Daughters of the American Revolution flag contest in 1925.

South Carolina

Designed in 1776 and officially adopted in 1861, the South Carolina flag has a blue background with a silver crescent. The design is taken from the uniforms of South Carolina's army troops. A palmetto tree was added later to represent Fort Moultrie. During the American Revolutionary War, Fort Moultrie was protected by palmetto logs. The wood was so strong that British cannonballs bounced off.

Tennessee

Tennessee's state flag was adopted in 1905. There are three stars on the flag. Each star represents the three parts of the state—east, middle, and west. These stars are bound to each other by a white band. The white band shows unbreakable unity of the state.

Texas

The Texas flag is called the Lone Star and was adopted in 1845. The colors on the flag are red, white, and blue. Red represents bravery, white stands for purity, and blue shows loyalty. The large white star was first used on the flag in the 1830s during battles between Texas and Mexico.

Virginia

In 1861, Virginia adopted its state flag. The flag includes the state seal on a blue background. The seal shows the goddess Virtue with a sword and spear. She is standing over a tyrant that she has defeated. Virtue represents Virgina, and the tyrant symbolizes Great Britian.

West Virginia

On June 20, 1863, West Virginia became a state. In 1929, it adopted a state flag. The state flag has a rock showing the date Virginia became a state on a white background. Farming and mining also are represented on the flag.

The Northeast

The Northeast is the smallest region in the United States. It is east of the Great Lakes and south of Canada. The Atlantic Ocean borders the Northeast's east coast. There are nine states in the Northeast. They are Connecticut, Maine, Massachusetts, New Hampshire, New Jersey, New York, Pennsylvania, Rhode Island, and Vermont.

Flags

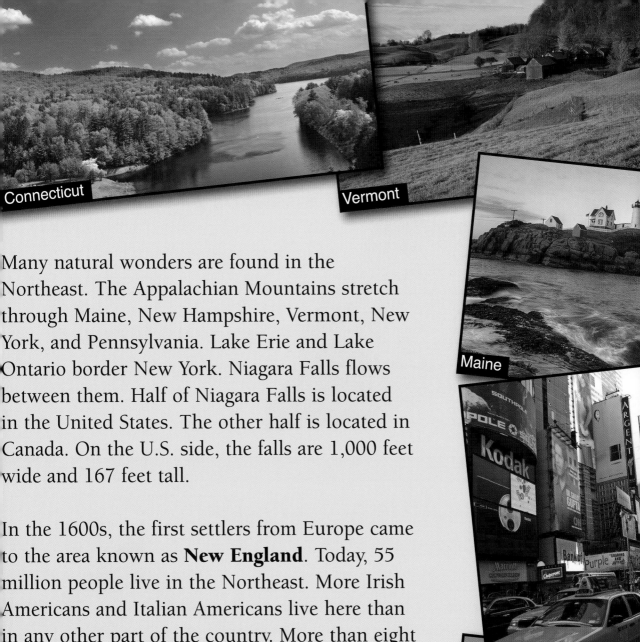

Connecticut

Vermont

Maine

New York

Many natural wonders are found in the Northeast. The Appalachian Mountains stretch through Maine, New Hampshire, Vermont, New York, and Pennsylvania. Lake Erie and Lake Ontario border New York. Niagara Falls flows between them. Half of Niagara Falls is located in the United States. The other half is located in Canada. On the U.S. side, the falls are 1,000 feet wide and 167 feet tall.

In the 1600s, the first settlers from Europe came to the area known as **New England**. Today, 55 million people live in the Northeast. More Irish Americans and Italian Americans live here than in any other part of the country. More than eight million people live in New York City, the largest city in the country.

Web Crawler

Learn more about New England at
www.discovernewengland.org.

See spectacular views of Niagara Falls at
www.niagarafallsstatepark.com/Destination_
PhotoGallery.aspx.

Pennsylvania

Connecticut

The Daughters of the American Revolution proposed the first state flag of Connecticut. A flag with blue and white colors was adopted in 1897. There is a shield of gold and silver, and a white streamer with the motto *Qui Transtulit Sustinet*, which is Latin for "He Who is Transplanted Still Sustains." This motto honors Connecticut's early settlers.

Maine

Maine chose its state flag in 1909. Maine's coat of arms is shown on a background of blue. The blue is the same shade as the blue in the national flag. The shield in the coat of arms has a pine tree and a moose. A farmer and a seaman represent the industries of Maine. The North Star surrounds the shield.

Massachusetts

The Massachusetts flag shows the state seal, which has an American Indian and a star. Underneath the seal is the phrase *Ense petit placidam sub libertate quietem*. This means "By the sword we seek peace, but peace only under liberty."

New Hampshire

The state flag of New Hampshire was designed in 1784 and was adopted in 1909. The flag pictures the state seal on a deep blue background. The seal has the ship *Raleigh* sailing near a large gray

granite rock. It is in front of a yellow Sun rising over blue water. The *Raleigh* was built to fight the British during the American Revolutionary War.

New Jersey

New Jersey's state flag has a buff background. This is the color of part of the uniform worn by General George Washington in 1779. In the center of the flag is the state coat of arms. The flag shows the goddesses of liberty and agriculture. They symbolize freedom and prosperity.

New York

Today's state flag for New York is a modern version of the American Revolutionary War flag. The coat of arms on the flag was adopted in 1778. The flag itself was adopted in 1901. The coat of arms shows figures representing liberty and justice. Above the shield is an eagle standing on a globe. A banner with the state motto is below the coat of arms. The banner reads *Excelsior*, which means "ever upward."

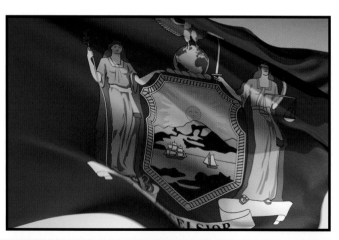

Pennsylvania

The first flag of Pennsylvania was adopted in 1907. The state coat of arms is on a blue background. The blue of the state flag matches the blue of the United States national flag.

Rhode Island

The Rhode Island state flag was adopted in 1897. The flag reads "Hope" in gold lettering on a blue ribbon. The flag is white, with yellow on three sides. A yellow anchor is circled by 13 yellow stars, symbolizing the original 13 colonies.

Vermont

Vermont used the United States' flag as a model for its flag design. This flag was first adopted in 1803. Then, a new flag was adopted in 1923.

The National Flag

National emblems are symbols that are used for the entire country. The rose, the official flower of the United States, is one such symbol. Another is the bald eagle, which is the the national bird. The oak tree is the national tree. The American flag, known as the star-spangled banner, is the national flag.

On June 4, 1777, the idea for a national flag was born. Flag Day is celebrated on June 4th every year.

In 1818, it was decided that there would be 13 stripes on the flag for the original states of the Union. There was also one star for every state that joined the Union. When a new state joined the Union, a star was added to the flag on July 4th of the year it joined.

In May 1776, three members from the Continental Congress came to the home of Betsy Ross. Those representatives were George Washington, Robert Morris, and George Ross. They asked Betsy to sew the first American flag.

History of the Flag

In 1831, Captain William Driver, a shipmaster from Salem, Massachusetts, left on one of his many world voyages. Friends gave him with a flag of 24 stars. As the banner opened to the ocean breeze, he exclaimed, "Old Glory." Driver kept his flag for many years, protecting it during the Civil War, until it was flown over the Tennessee capital. "Old Glory" became a nickname for the national flag.

Guide to State Flags

THE NATIONAL FLAG
September 11, 1775

ALABAMA
Adopted: 1895

ALASKA
Adopted: 1959

ARIZONA
Adopted: 1927

ARKANSAS
Adopted: 1926

CALIFORNIA
Adopted: 1911

COLORADO
Adopted: 1911

CONNECTICUT
Adopted: 1897

DELAWARE
Adopted: 1913

FLORIDA
Adopted: 1900

GEORGIA
Adopted: 2004

HAWAI'I
Adopted: 1845

IDAHO
Adopted: 1927

ILLINOIS
Adopted: 1970

INDIANA
Adopted: 1917

IOWA
Adopted: 1921

KANSAS
Adopted: 1925

KENTUCKY
Adopted: 1928

LOUISIANA
Adopted: 1912

MAINE
Adopted: 1909

MARYLAND
Adopted: 1904

 **MASSACHUSETTS**
Adopted: 1970

 MICHIGAN
Adopted: 1911

 **MINNESOTA**
Adopted: 1893

 **MISSISSIPPI**
Adopted: 1894

 MISSOURI
Adopted: 1913

 **MONTANA**
Adopted: 1905

 **NEBRASKA**
Adopted: 1925

 **NEVADA**
Adopted: 1929

 **NEW HAMPSHIRE**
Adopted: 1909

 **NEW JERSEY**
Adopted: 1896

 NEW MEXICO
Adopted: 1923

 NEW YORK
Adopted: 1901

 **NORTH CAROLINA**
Adopted: 1885

 NORTH DAKOTA
Adopted: 1911

 **OHIO**
Adopted: 1902

 **OKLAHOMA**
Adopted: 1925

 **OREGON**
Adopted: 1923

 PENNSYLVANIA
Adopted: 1907

 **RHODE ISLAND**
Adopted: 1897

 **SOUTH CAROLINA**
Adopted: 1861

 **SOUTH DAKOTA**
Adopted: 1909

 **TENNESSEE**
Adopted: 1905

 **TEXAS**
Adopted: 1845

 **UTAH**
Adopted: 1913

 **VERMONT**
Adopted: 1923

 VIRGINIA
Adopted: 1861

 **WASHINGTON**
Adopted: 1923

 **WEST VIRGINIA**
Adopted: 1929

 WISCONSIN
Adopted: 1913

 **WYOMING**
Adopted: 1917

Parts of the Flag

The American flag is more than 200 years old. Through the years it has inspired nationalism, hope, and pride. The national flag has many nicknames, including the stars and stripes, Old Glory, and the star-spangled banner.

STRIPES

There are 13 stripes on the national flag. They represent the original 13 states to join the Union. The idea of using stripes came from the flag of Captain Abraham Markoe's Philadelphia Light Horse Troop in 1775. That flag had 13 blue and silver stripes.

BLUE Blue signifies watchfulness, perseverance, and justice.

STARS Stars were used to represent people's desire to achieve greatness. The common metaphor "reaching for the stars" developed from this idea.

RED The color red in the stripes stands for courage, hardwork, and valor. It also signifies the red of the British flag.

WHITE White symbolizes purity and innocence. The white stripes signifies the beginning of life in a new country.

Test Your Knowledge

1 Which state flags were adopted in 1911?

2 Which flag has a different emblem on both the back and the front?

3 What does the number 13 mean to Americans?

4 What type of tree is in the design of South Carolina's state flag?
a. blue spruce
b. saw palmetto
c. American elm
d. oak
e. pinyon pine

5 Virginia's state flag depicts which goddess?

6 What do the colors in the U.S. flag stand for?

7 Which two state flags were inspired by General George Washington?
a. Alaska and Florida
b. Rhode Island and Idaho
c. Delaware and New Jersey
d. Texas and Nevada

8 What does *l'etoile du nord* mean in French?

9 Which flags have the St. Andrew's cross incorporated into their design?
   a. Alabama and Florida
   b. Montana and New York
   c. Washington and Alaska
   d. Ohio and Hawai'i
   e. Idaho and Texas

13 Which is the only flag shaped like a burgee?

14 Who sewed the first American Flag?

10 Which state flag was given to a king?

15 Which state flags were adopted in 1923?

11 Which states have the North Star on their flag?
   a. New Mexico and Wyoming
   b. Vermont and Kansas
   c. Utah and Tennessee
   d. Minnesota and Maine
   e. Illinois and Virginia

12 What animal is on Missouri's state flag?

Create Your Own Flag

Work together with a friend to design your own flag. You can start by thinking about what might be important symbols to include. What are important ideals for you follow? What symbols might represent you? What are the activities that you are involved in at your school? Is there an important date for you, a day that something significant happened?

Then, think about the colors that would best suit you and your friend. Will you have a flag with one main section, like the flag of Alaska? Maybe it will be broken up into different sections with varying patterns, like the stars and stripes on the American flag? Would there be one main color or a few different colors? What do those colors mean to you?

As a pair, make your flag. When you are done with the artwork, make sure to include a description of the parts of your flag. Explain why you chose the symbols and colors that you did.

Further Research

Many books and websites provide information on state flags. To learn more about flags, borrow books from the library, or surf the Internet.

Books

Most libraries have computers that connect to a database for researching information. If you input a key word, you will be provided with a list of books in the library that contain information on that topic. Non-fiction books are arranged numerically, using their call number. Fiction books are organized alphabetically by the author's last name.

Websites

Find fun facts about each of the 50 U.S. states by clicking on this map from the U.S. Census Bureau **www.census.gov/schools/facts**.

Learn about flags and forests at **http://ecokids.earthday.ca/pub/eco_info/topics/forests/index.cfm**.

Read more about the regions of the United States at **www.factmonster.com/ipka/A0770177.html**.

Play online flag games and activities at **www.va.gov/kids/K-5/multicontent.asp?intPageId=8**.

Glossary

Big Dipper: a group of stars that resembles a large spoon

bottony: a cross with each arm ending in a three-leaf clover shape

Confederate Battle Flag: the flag under which the Union Army joined together as the Confederacy, fought under during the American Revolutionary War

conquistador: 16th century Spanish conquerors

Daughters of the American Revolution: a historical group for women who have had one or more ancestors who served in the American Revolutionary War

Great Plains: a vast grassland region covering 10 U.S. states and 4 Canadian provinces. Used for farming and raising cattle

Louisiana Purchase: a treaty signed with France in 1803 in which the United States bought the land extending from the Mississippi River to the Rocky Mountains and from Canada to the Gulf of Mexico

New England: the most northeastern U.S. states—Connecticut, Rhode Island, Massachusetts, New Hampshire, Vermont, and Maine

Polaris: the North Star; the brightest star in the sky

Union Jack: Great Britain's flag

Index